OCEANS ALIVE

Swordfish

by Colleen Sexton

BELLWETHER MEDIA • MINNEAPOLIS, MN

BLASTOFF! READERS 2

Note to Librarians, Teachers, and Parents:

Blastoff! Readers are carefully developed by literacy experts and combine standards-based content with developmentally appropriate text.

Level 1 provides the most support through repetition of high-frequency words, light text, predictable sentence patterns, and strong visual support.

Level 2 offers early readers a bit more challenge through varied simple sentences, increased text load, and less repetition of high-frequency words.

Level 3 advances early-fluent readers toward fluency through increased text and concept load, less reliance on visuals, longer sentences, and more literary language.

Level 4 builds reading stamina by providing more text per page, increased use of punctuation, greater variation in sentence patterns, and increasingly challenging vocabulary.

Level 5 encourages children to move from "learning to read" to "reading to learn" by providing even more text, varied writing styles, and less familiar topics.

Whichever book is right for your reader, Blastoff! Readers are the perfect books to build confidence and encourage a love of reading that will last a lifetime!

This edition first published in 2009 by Bellwether Media, Inc.

No part of this publication may be reproduced in whole or in part without written permission of the publisher. For information regarding permission, write to Bellwether Media, Inc., Attention: Permissions Department, Post Office Box 19349, Minneapolis, MN 55419.

Library of Congress Cataloging-in-Publication Data
Sexton, Colleen A., 1967–
  Swordfish / by Colleen Sexton.
    p. cm. – (Blastoff! readers. Oceans alive)
  Includes bibliographical references and index.
  Summary: "Simple text and supportive images introduce beginning readers to swordfish. Intended for students in kindergarten through third grade"–Provided by publisher.
  ISBN-13: 978-1-60014-253-6 (hardcover : alk. paper)
  ISBN-10: 1-60014-253-2 (hardcover : alk. paper)
  1. Swordfish–Juvenile literature. I. Title.

QL638.X5S49 2009
597'.78–dc22   2008033544

Contents

Swordfish **migrate**. They swim to cool waters in summer and to warm waters in winter.

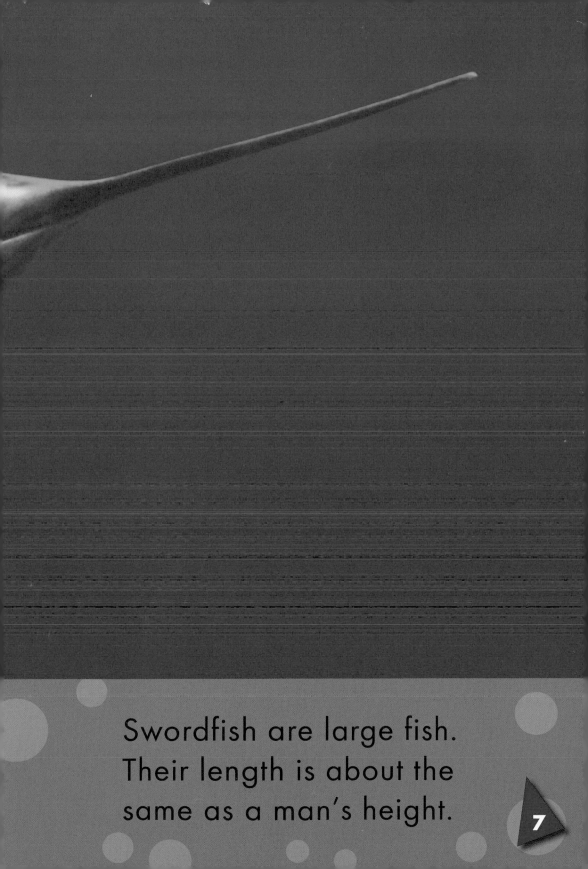

Swordfish are large fish.
Their length is about the
same as a man's height.

fin

Swordfish can be blue, gray, black, or brown. Their bellies are white or silver.

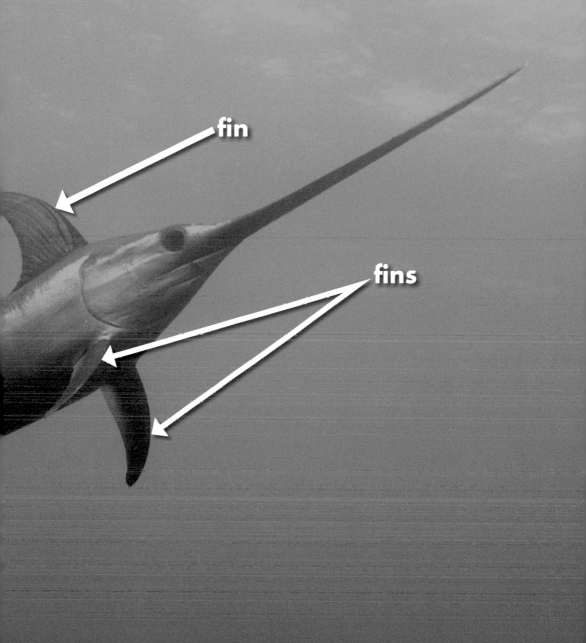

fin

fins

Swordfish have **fins** and a tail. They move their tail and fins to swim.

Young swordfish have **scales** and teeth. Swordfish lose their scales and teeth as they grow.

10

Adult swordfish have smooth skin that helps them glide through the water.

Swordfish have large eyes.

Their large eyes make them good hunters.

gills

Swordfish breathe through **gills**.

Swordfish get their name from their long top jaw. It ends in a point and looks like a sword.

Swordfish use this jaw to fight off sharks, whales, and other **predators**.

Swordfish mainly use their sword to hunt for food. They eat small fish that swim in **schools**.

Swordfish rush into a school of
fish to hunt. They move their
sword back and forth to stun fish.

Then swordfish eat the fish
that are hurt.

Swordfish often come close to the surface to **bask** in the sun.

Sometimes they jump
high out of the water.
What a sight!

Glossary

bask—to lie in the heat of the sun

fins—flaps on a fish's body used for moving, steering, and stopping in the water

gills—organs near the mouth that a fish uses to breathe; the gills move oxygen from the water to the fish's blood.

migrate—to move from place to place with the seasons

predator—an animal that hunts other animals for food

scales—small, hard plates that cover the bodies of many fish

school—a large number of fish that swim and feed together

To Learn More

AT THE LIBRARY

Coldiron, Deborah. *Swordfish*. Edina, Minn.: ABDO, 2008.

Korman, Susan. *Swordfish Returns*. Norwalk, Conn.: Soundprints, 2003.

Sill, Cathryn P. *About Fish: A Guide for Children*. Atlanta, Ga.: Peachtree, 2002.

ON THE WEB

Learning more about swordfish is as easy as 1, 2, 3.

1. Go to www.factsurfer.com.

2. Enter "swordfish" into the search box.

3. Click the "Surf" button and you will see a list of related Web sites.

With factsurfer.com, finding more information is just a click away.

Index

The images in this book are reproduced through the courtesy of: Brian J. Skerry / Getty Images, front cover, p. 11; Stawek, pp. 4-5; Eleanora de Sabata / Sea Pics, pp. 6-7; Getty Images, pp. 8-9,10,18-19, 20; Franco Banfi / Sea Pics, pp. 12-13; Ronald C. Modra / Sports Imagery / Getty Images, pp. 14-15, 21; Marc Chamberlain / Alamy, p. 16; Annetje, p. 17.